Wood Pellet Smoker and Grill Cookbook 2021

The Ultimate Guide to Master the Barbecue Like A Pro With Tasty and Easy Recipes

John Paul Smith

Table Of Contents

Introduction

A pellet grill is a multi-functional grill designed to use compressed wood pellets as its fuel. These innovative cookers combine the different striking elements of smokers, gas grills, ovens, and even charcoal. By varying the kind of wood pellet, you are using, you can bring in the variation in the actual flavor of the food. This book will introduce you to various food recipe that you can do using meat, seafoods, poultry and vegetables. This Ultimate Guide for Wood Pellet Smoker and Grill Cookbook is designed so that you can use it whenever and wherever the occasion demands. Feel free to browse forward to recipes you are interested in. It is formatted in a uniform way that shows each recipe's preparation time, cooking time, number of servings, the different ingredients you will need, step-by-step direction and nutritional contents, in that order, respectively.

A little hard-core research reveals that there are some companies still in business today that might appear to have the first to offer the first pellet-style smokers to the open market. Dating back to the early 1980s, these companies first experimented with wood pellets as fuel for barbecue smokers. As they progressed with the designs, many successful grills were built and tested, and the rest was history.

So, what exactly is a wood Pellet Smoker Grill? Here are the basics of an excellent high-quality wood pellet smoker. Generally, the higher the temperature gauge is set, the more pellets get dispensed into the drill. After the pellets are delivered into the fire pot, a red-hot rod will ignite them, which starts the flames. A fan then keeps a gentle airflow across the fire area that creates a convection oven type of heat that cooks your food nicely and evenly. A drip tray is located just over the fire pot to keep you clear of any direct flame activity. This tray also catches any subsequent drippings to help prevent unwanted flare-ups.

The design technology behind wood Pellet Smoker Grills is not new. Still, the grills are indeed making a lively splash in the grill markets. People are asking if these types of grills are safe to use. The answer is yes. Food-grade wood pellets are not any riskier than any other food prep choices.

The wood pellets used in pellet smokers are exclusive to that task. This is because they produce less than 1% ash. As an example, if you use an entire 40-pound bag of pellets in your smoker, unbelievably, you will only have ½ of a cup of ash, which is only a half a cup for 40 lb. bag. In addition to this, they provide diners with gigantic flavor per capita and no worries about the need to watch the levels of air to fuel mixture, like you would when using wood chips or wood chunks.

How the Heat Distribution Works in Pellet Smoker Grills?

A heat shield that covers the firebox works to distribute the heat to both sides of the grill. This causes the air to flow up into the convection-style grill chamber. Then, a sensor that is conveniently mounted on the inside of the grill sends data electronically to the on-board computer at the fantastic rate of 10 times per second. The controller then adjusts both the airflow and the pellet distribution mechanism to maintain the temperature that you set.

Why Pellet Grills?

Cooking on a pellet grill is a new and unique experience. By utilizing hardwood pellets, the meat product gets infused with a real woodsy, smoky flavor. The new Pellet Smoker Grills can be relied on to do the work on their own, as they are set up to be automatic by the user.

The primary and most obvious difference is that they provide the user with an automated air and fuel delivery system, making a pellet grill much more comfortable to control temperatures and relax while doing it.

So, if you thought that smokers are just too challenging to control cooking temperatures, well think again. Pellet grills simply remove the fuss and worry that traditional smokers require, making them virtually a "set it and forget it" way to grill.

Pellet grills give you even more as if that were not enough. With your new pellet grill, you have the absolute convenience of combining several varied cooking options. Old-time smokers only smoke their food, so if you want to grill, bake, and roast your food, you will need to purchase separate units for each process.

Pellet Grills are different than propane or gas grills in that they offer more control. Pellet grills and gas grills both offer their own set of convenient features to the outdoor chef. Still, they look more closely, and you will see some significant differences. Gas grills are excellent when cooking chores, but due to poor insulation, they do not typically perform very well at all at low cooking temperatures. Also, the older style of propane grills needs to be set up so that they receive the proper degree of ventilation. This, alone, makes them a poor choice for smokers. The Pellet Grill is a no brainer in today's world!

Pellet grills provide the chef with more flavor options. With pellet grills, the wood pellets are available in many different flavors. This provides you with the ability to cook all the foods on your Pellet Smoker Grill. In the end, sure, they both cook your food, but the pellet grill is exponentially better on so many levels. For me, there is no choice but to the Pellet Smoker Grill!

Then there is the question of using a Pellet Grill or staying with the highly coveted charcoal method of barbecuing you are fine foods.

Charcoal grills have long been considered the king of the backyard barbecue area. There are several choices of configurations for charcoal grills but with two choices for fuel: lump charcoal or charcoal briquettes. Grilling using a charcoal grill is definitely a labor of love. I know several people who defend them to the ends of the earth, and that's fine. We are all different, and thank goodness for that, too. But cooking on a charcoal grill is really not so easy. It takes quite a lot of practice to get all the elements just right and is difficult to control temperatures.

The way pellet grills are used when grilling and smoking are infinitely more straightforward. This is precisely why they have become the nation's number one seller. As for the cleanup, have you ever seen a charcoal grill the next morning? You may need to carry them out to the trash or recycling. It's not the same with your pellet grill, though. Absolutely simple cleanup is assured for each cooking adventure when you cook with pellets.

Chapter 1: Breakfast Recipes

1. Fruit Crisps

Preparation time: 20 minutes

Cooking time: 35 minutes

Servings: 2-4

Ingredients:

Whipped Cream

2 - 3 tsp. Cane Sugar, raw

½ tsp. of Vanilla

2 - 3 lb. Pears or Apples, cored, peeled and chopped

12 tbsp. Butter, unsalted

¼ tsp. Nutmeg, ground

½ tsp. of Salt +1/8 tsp.

1 tsp. Cinnamon, ground

¾ cup brown sugar, packed

½ cup of Almond Flour

1 cup Flour

2 cups Rolled oats

Pellet: Cherry

Directions:

Preheat the grill to 350F with closed lid.

Place a parchment paper on a baking dish. Place 8 ramekins (1 - cup size).

First combine the nutmeg, salt, cinnamon, brown sugar, flours, and oats.

Add butter and cut it into small pieces using a fork.

Now in a bowl combine 1/8 tsp. Salt, vanilla and fruit. Taste and adjust according to your taste with the cane sugar.

Fill the ramekins with fruit and then sprinkle with the crispy topping (3 tbsp.). Place the baking dish on the grill.

Bake for 35 minutes. Let it rest 20 minutes before serving.

Serve topped with whipped cream and enjoy!

Nutrition:

Calories: 102

Proteins: 2g

Carbs: 22g

Fat: 2g

2. Baked French Toast

Preparation time: 20 minutes

Cooking time: 1 hour

Servings: 2-4

Ingredients:

12 Eggs

1 cup Blueberries, fresh, rinsed

½ cup Sugar

1 cup of Sour cream

12 oz. softened Cream Cheese

1 Loaf of bread, French or Italian, a day old, cut into cubes (1 - inch)

1 tsp. of Vanilla Extract

½ cup of Maple Syrup

2 cups of Milk

½ tsp. salt

Pellet: Apple

Directions:

Preheat the grill to 350F with closed lid.

Grease a baking dish (9x13 inch). Place ½ of the bread cubes.

In a bowl combine the sugar, sour cream and cream cheese. Mix with a handheld mixer. Spread over the cubes with a spatula.

Sprinkle with 1 cup of Blueberries and place the other half of the bread cubes.

In another bowl whisk the syrup, milk, eggs, salt and vanilla extract.

Cover the dish with a foil and place in the fridge. Refrigerate overnight. Let is sit for 30 minutes before cooking.

Bake in a closed grill for about 30 minutes.

Now remove the foil and cook for 30 minutes more.

Serve as it is or topped with whipped cream and syrup. Enjoy!

Nutrition:

Calories: 480

Proteins: 15g

Carbs: 70g

Fat: 24g

Chapter 2: Beef Recipes

3. Honey Glazed Smoked Beef

Preparation Time: 10 minutes

Cooking Time: 8 hours

Servings: 10

Ingredients:

1 6-pound beef brisket

2 ½ tablespoons salt

2 ½ tablespoons pepper

¾ cup barbecue sauce

3 tablespoons red wine

3 tablespoons raw honey

Directions:

Preheat the smoker to 225°F (107°C). Spread the charcoal on one side.

Meanwhile, rub the beef brisket with salt, pepper, and barbecue sauce.

When the smoker has reached the desired temperature, place the brisket on the grill with the fat side up. Splash red wine over beef brisket.

Smoke the beef brisket for 8 hours. Check the smoker every 2 hours and add more charcoal if it is necessary.

Once it is done, take the smoked beef brisket from the smoker then transfers to a serving dish.

Drizzle raw honey over the beef and let it sit for about an hour before slicing.

Serve with roasted or sautéed vegetables according to your desire.

Nutrition:

Calories: 90

Carbs: 8g

Fat: 1g

Protein: 11g

4. Spiced Smoked Beef with Oregano

Preparation Time: 10 minutes

Cooking Time: 8 hours

Servings: 10

Ingredients:

1 8-pounduntrimmed brisket

6 tablespoons paprika

¼ cup salt

3 tablespoons garlic powder

2 tablespoons onion powder

1 ½ tablespoons black pepper

1 ½ tablespoons dried parsley

2 ½ teaspoons cayenne pepper

2 ½ teaspoons cumin

1 ½ teaspoons coriander

2 teaspoons oregano

½ teaspoon hot chili powder

Preheat the smoker prior to smoking.

Add woodchips during the smoking time.

Directions:

Cook the brisket for 6 hours.

After 6 hours, usually the smoker temperature decreases to 170°F (77°C).

Take the brisket out from the smoker then wrap with aluminum foil.

Return the brisket to the smoker then cooks again for 2 hours—this will increase the tenderness of the smoked beef.

Once it is done, remove the smoked beef from the smoker then place in a serving dish.

Cut the smoked beef into slices then enjoy!

Nutrition:

Calories: 267

Carbs: 0g

Fat: 21g

Protein: 20g

5. BBQ Sweet Pepper Meatloaf

Preparation time: 20 minutes

Cooking time: 3 hours and 15 minutes

Servings: 8

Ingredients:

1 cup chopped red sweet peppers

5 pounds ground beef

1 cup chopped green onion

1 tablespoon salt

1 tablespoon ground black pepper

1 cup panko breadcrumbs

2 tablespoon BBQ rub and more as needed

1 cup ketchup

2 eggs

Directions:

Switch on the Traeger grill, fill the grill hopper with Texas beef blend flavored wood pellets, power the grill on by using the control panel, select 'smoke' on the temperature dial, or set the temperature to 225 degrees F and let it preheat for a minimum of 5 minutes.

Meanwhile, take a large bowl, place all the ingredients in it except for ketchup and then stir until well combined.

Shape the mixture into meatloaf and then sprinkle with some BBQ rub.

When the grill has preheated, open the lid, place meatloaf on the grill grate, shut the grill, and smoke for 2 hours and 15 minutes.

Then change the smoking temperature to 375 degrees F, insert a food thermometer into the meatloaf and cook for 45 minutes or more until the internal temperature of meatloaf reaches 155 degrees F.

Brush the top of meatloaf with ketchup and then continue cooking for 15 minutes until glazed.

When done, transfer food to a dish, let it rest for 10 minutes, then cut it into slices and serve.

Nutrition:

Nutrition:

Calories: 160.5 Cal

Fat: 2.8 g

Carbs: 13.2 g

Protein: 17.2 g

Fiber: 1 g

6. Blackened Steak

Preparation time: 10 minutes

Cooking time: 60 minutes

Servings: 4

Ingredients:

2 steaks, each about 40 ounces

4 tablespoons blackened rub

4 tablespoons butter, unsalted

Directions:

Switch on the Traeger grill, fill the grill hopper with hickory flavored wood pellets, power the grill on by using the control panel, select 'smoke' on the temperature dial, or set the temperature to 225 degrees F and let it preheat for a minimum of 15 minutes.

Transfer steaks to a dish and then repeat with the remaining steak.

Let seared steaks rest for 10 minutes, then slice each steak across the grain and serve.

Nutrition:

Calories: 184.4 Cal

Fat: 8.8 g

Carbs: 0 g Protein: 23.5 g

7. BBQ Brisket

Preparation time: 12 hours

Cooking time: 10 hours

Servings: 8

Ingredients:

1 beef brisket, about 12 pounds

Beef rub as needed

Directions:

Season beef brisket with beef rub until well coated, place it in a large plastic bag, seal it and let it marinate for a minimum of 12 hours in the refrigerator.

When ready to cook, switch on the Traeger grill, fill the grill hopper with hickory flavored wood pellets, power the grill on by using the control panel, select 'smoke' on the temperature dial, or set the temperature to 225 degrees F and let it preheat for a minimum of 15 minutes.

When the grill has preheated, open the lid, place marinated brisket on the grill grate fat-side down, shut the grill, and smoke for 6 hours until the internal temperature reaches 160 degrees F.Then wrap the brisket in foil, return it back to the grill grate and cook for 4 hours until the internal temperature reaches 204 degrees F.When done, transfer brisket to a cutting board, let it rest for 30 minutes, then cut it into slices and serve.

Nutrition: Calories: 328 Cal Fat: 21 g Protein: 32 g

8. Prime Rib Roast

Preparation time: 24 hours

Cooking time: 4 hours and 30 minutes

Servings: 8

Ingredients:

1 prime rib roast, containing 5 to 7 bones

Rib rub as needed

Directions:

Season rib roast with rib rub until well coated, place it in a large plastic bag, seal it and let it marinate for a minimum of 24 hours in the refrigerator.

When ready to cook, switch on the Traeger grill, fill the grill hopper with cherry flavored wood pellets, power the grill on by using the control panel, select 'smoke' on the temperature dial, or set the temperature to 225 degrees F and let it preheat for a minimum of 15 minutes.

When the grill has preheated, open the lid, place rib roast on the grill grate fat-side up, change the smoking temperature to 425 degrees F, shut the grill, and smoke for 30 minutes.

Then change the smoking temperature to 325 degrees F and continue cooking for 3 to 4 hours until roast has cooked to the desired level, rare at 120 degrees F, medium rare at 130 degrees F, medium at 140 degrees F, and well done at 150 degrees F.

When done, transfer roast rib to a cutting board, let it rest for 15 minutes, then cut it into slices and serve.

Nutrition:

Calories: 248 Cal

Fat: 21.2 g

Protein: 28 g

9. Thai Beef Skewers

Preparation time: 15 minutes

Cooking time: 8 minutes

Servings: 6

Ingredients:

½ of medium red bell pepper, destemmed, cored, cut into a ¼-inch piece

½ of beef sirloin, fat trimmed

½ cup salted peanuts, roasted, chopped

1 teaspoon minced garlic

1 tablespoon grated ginger

1 lime, juiced

1 teaspoon ground black pepper

1 tablespoon sugar

1/4 cup soy sauce

1/4 cup olive oil

Directions:

Prepare the marinade and for this, take a small bowl, place all of its ingredients in it, whisk until combined, and then pour it into a large plastic bag.

Cut into beef sirloin 1-1/4-inch dice, add to the plastic bag containing marinade, seal the bag, turn it upside down to coat beef pieces with the marinade and let it marinate for a minimum of 2 hours in the refrigerator.

When ready to cook, switch on the Traeger grill, fill the grill hopper with cherry flavored wood pellets, power the grill on by using the control panel, select 'smoke' on the temperature dial, or set the temperature to 425 degrees F and let it preheat for a minimum of 5 minutes.

Meanwhile, remove beef pieces from the marinade and then thread onto skewers.

When the grill has preheated, open the lid, place prepared skewers on the grill grate, shut the grill, and smoke for 4 minutes per side until done.

When done, transfer skewers to a dish, sprinkle with peanuts and red pepper, and then serve.

Nutrition:

Calories: 124 Cal

Fat: 5.5 g

Carbs: 1.7 g

Protein: 15.6 g

Fiber: 0 g

Chapter 3: Pork Recipes

10. Smoked Spicy Pork Medallions

Preparation time: 15 minutes

Cooking time: 1 hour 30 minutes

Servings: 6

Ingredients:

2 lbs. pork medallions

3/4 cup chicken stock

1/2 cup tomato sauce (organic)

2 Tbs of smoked hot paprika (or to taste)

2 Tbsp of fresh basil finely chopped

1 Tbsp oregano

Salt and pepper to taste

Directions:

In a bowl, combine together the chicken stock, tomato sauce, paprika, oregano, salt, and pepper.

Brush generously over the outside of the tenderloin.

Start the pellet grill on Smoke with the lid open until the fire is established (4 to 5 minutes). Set the temperature to 250°F and preheat, lid closed, for 10 to 15 minutes.

Place the pork on the grill grate and smoke until the internal temperature of the pork is at least medium-rare (about 145°F), for 1 1/2 hours.

Let meat rest for 15 minutes and serve.

Nutrition:

Calories: 364.2

Carbs: 4g

Fat: 14.4g

Fiber: 2g

Protein: 52.4g

11. Smoked Pork Loin

Preparation time: 30 minutes

Cooking time: 2 hours 30 minutes

Servings: 8

Ingredients:

4 pounds of pork loin, trimmed

4 tablespoons olive oil

2 tablespoons garlic powder

2 tablespoons rosemary, dried and chopped

½ teaspoon of salt, or to taste

1 cup dry pistachios, chopped and roasted

1 tablespoon ground black pepper

Directions:

Preheat the smoker grill for 50 minutes at 270 degrees Fahrenheit.

Coat the pork with a generous amount of olive oil.

Next rub the pork with garlic powder, rosemary, salt, pistachio, and black pepper.

Put the pork directly onto the grill grate and smoke it for 3 hours by closing the lid.

Once the internal temperature reaches 150 degrees Fahrenheit the pork is ready to be served.

Enjoy.

Nutrition:

Calories: 143 kCal

Fat: 5.7 g

Protein: 21 g

12. Smoked Pork Shoulder

Preparation time: 30 minutes

Cooking time: 1 hour 30 minutes

Servings: 6

Ingredients:

3 pounds pork shoulder, roasts

Shoulder Rub Ingredients

1/4 cup brown sugar

¼ cup white sugar

1 tablespoon paprika

1 tablespoon garlic powder

Salt, to taste

½ tablespoon chili powder

1 teaspoon cayenne pepper

¼ teaspoon black pepper

2 teaspoons dried oregano

2 teaspoons cumin

Liquid Ingredients to Be Injected

3/4 cup apple juice

1 cup of water

1/2 cup sugar

Salt, to taste

6 tablespoons Worcestershire sauce

Directions:

Take a large bowl and add all the shoulder spice rub ingredients and mix well.

Take a separate bowl and add all the liquid ingredients.

Now use an injector to inject the mixed liquid into the meat.

Pat dry it from the top with a paper towel.

Rub the spice mixture on top and left for a few hours before cooking.

Preheat the smoker grill for 50 minutes at 220 degrees F.

Put the meat onto the grill grate and cook for 2 hours at 225 degrees.

Serve and enjoy.

Nutrition:

Calories: 236 kCal

Protein: 17 g

Fat: 18 g

13. Zesty Herbal Smoke Pork Tenderloin

Preparation time: 30 minutes

Cooking time: 3 hours

Servings: 4

Ingredients:

2-4 pork tenderloins

6 tablespoons of BBQ sauce

Pork Rub Ingredients

The ½ cup of cane sugar

⅓ teaspoon of chili powder

¼ tablespoon of granulated onion

½ tablespoon of granulated garlic

1 tablespoon of dried chilies

1 tablespoon of dill weed

1 tablespoon of lemon powder

1 tablespoon mustard powder

Directions:

Take a large mixing bowl and combine all the poke rub ingredients in it.

Now preheat the smoker grill at 225 degrees Fahrenheit until the smoke started to form

Cooking Time for 3 hours, until the internal temperature reaches 150 degrees Fahrenheit.

After 3 hours a brush generous amount of the barbecue sauce and then left it to sit for 20 minutes before serving.

Serve and enjoy.

Nutrition:

Calories: 147 kCal

Protein: 26 g

Fat: 4 g

14. Pulled Hickory-Smoked Pork Butts

Preparation time: 30 to 45 minutes

Cooking time: 6 hours

Servings: 20

Ingredients:

Pellet: Hickory

2 (10-pound) boneless pork butts, vacuum-stuffed or fresh

1 cup roasted garlic–seasoned extra-virgin olive oil

¾ cup Pork Dry Rub, Jan's Original Dry Rub, or your preferred pork rub

Directions:

Trim the fat cap and any effectively available enormous segments of abundance fat from every pork butt as you see fit.

Remove the pork butts from the grill and double wrap everyone in heavy-duty aluminum foil. Take care to ensure that you keep your meat probes in the butts as you double-wrap them.

Return the wrapped pork butts to your 350°F pellet smoker-grill.

Keep cooking the foil-wrapped pork butts until the internal temperature of the pork butts arrives at 200°F to 205°F.

Remove the pork butts and FTC them for 3 to 4 hours before pulling and serving.

Force the smoked pork butts into minimal succulent shreds utilizing your preferred pulling technique. I prefer utilizing my hands while wearing heat-safe gloves.

On the off chance that you'd like, blend the pulled pork butts with any remaining fluids.

Serve the pulled pork with grill sauce on a fresh-prepared move topped with coleslaw, or serve the pulled pork with fixings like lettuce, tomato, red onion, mayo, cheese, and horseradish.

Nutrition:

Calories: 267 kCal

Protein: 25 g

Fat: 18 g

15. Pork Sirloin Tip Roast Three Ways

Preparation time: 20 minutes

Cooking time: 1½ to 3 hours

Servings: 4 to 6

Ingredients:

Pellet: Apple, Hickory

Apple-injected Roasted Pork Sirloin Tip Roast

1 (1½ to 2-pound) pork sirloin tip roast

¾ cup 100% apple juice

2 tablespoons roasted garlic–seasoned extra-virgin olive oil

5 tablespoons Pork Dry Rub or a business rub, for example, Plowboys BBQ Bovine Bold

Directions:

Dry the roast with a piece of paper

Utilize a flavor/marinade injector to infuse all zones of tip roast with the apple juice.

Rub the whole roast with the olive oil and afterward cover generously with the rub.

Utilize 2 silicone nourishment grade cooking groups or butcher's twine to support the roast.

Roast the meat until the internal temperature arrives at 145°F, about 1½ hours.

Rest the roast under a free foil tent for 15 minutes.

Remove the cooking groups or twine and cut the roast contrary to what would be expected.

Nutrition:

Calories: 354 kCal

Protein: 22 g

Fat: 30 g

16. Teriyaki-Marinated Pork Sirloin Tip Roast

Preparation time: 45 minutes

Cooking time: 2 hours 30 minutes

Ingredients:

1 (1½ to 2-pound) pork sirloin tip roast

Teriyaki marinade, for example, Mr. Yoshida's Original Gourmet Marinade

Directions:

Dry the roast with a piece of paper

Utilizing a 1-gallon cooler stockpiling sack or a sealable compartment, spread the roast with the teriyaki marinade.

Refrigerate medium-term, turning at regular intervals whenever the situation allows.

Smoke the meat for 1 hour at 180°F.

After 60 minutes, increase your pit temperature to 325°F.

Cook the roast until the internal temperature, at the thickest part of the roast, arrives at 145°F, around 1 to 1½ hours.

Rest the roast under a free foil tent for 15 minutes.

Remove the cooking groups or twine and cut the roast contrary to what would be expected.

Nutrition: Calories: 214 kCal Protein: 17 g Fat: 19 g

17. Hickory-Smoked Pork Sirloin Tip Roast

Preparation time: 30 minutes

Cooking time: 3 hours

Ingredients:

1 (1½ to 2-pound) pork sirloin tip roast

2 tablespoons roasted garlic–seasoned extra-virgin olive oil

5 tablespoons Jan's Original Dry Rub, Pork Dry Rub, or your preferred pork rub

Directions:

Pat the roast dry with a paper towel.

Rub the whole roast with the olive oil. Coat the roast with the rub.

Support the roast utilizing 2 to 3 silicone nourishment grade cooking groups or butcher's twine to ensure the roast keeps up its shape during cooking.

Wrap the tip roast in plastic wrap and refrigerate medium-term.

Place the roast directly on the grill grates and smoke the roast until the internal temperature, at the thickest part of the roast, arrives at 145°F, around 3 hours.Rest the roast under a free foil tent for 15 minutes.Remove the cooking groups or twine and cut the roast contrary to what would be expected.

Nutrition: Calories: 276 kCal Protein: 28 g Fat: 12 g

18. Double-Smoked Ham

Preparation time: 15 minutes

Cooking time: 2½ to 3 hours

Servings: 8 to 12

Ingredients:

Pellet: Apple, Hickory

1 (10-pound) applewood-smoked, boneless, wholly cooked, ready-to-eat ham or bone-in smoked ham

Directions:

Remove the ham from its bundling and let sit at room temperature for 30 minutes.

Arrange the wood pellet smoker-grill for a non-direct cooking and preheat to 180°F utilizing apple or hickory pellets relying upon what sort of wood was utilized for the underlying smoking.

Place the ham directly on the grill grates and smoke the ham for 1 hour at 180°F.After 60 minutes, increase pit temperature to 350°F.Cooking Time the ham until the internal temperature arrives at 140°F, about 1½ to 2 additional hours.Remove the ham and wrap in foil for 15 minutes before cutting contrary to what would be expected.

Nutrition: Calories: 215 kCal Protein: 21 g Fat: 19 g

Chapter 4: Lamb Recipes

19. Roast Lamb Leg

Preparation time: 15 minutes

Cooking time: 1 hour 15 minutes

Servings: 6

Ingredients:

Lamb leg with bone in – 7lbs

Garlic cloves – 8

Fresh rosemary sprigs – 2

Fresh oregano – 1

Juiced lemon – 1

Olive oil – 6 tablespoons

Freshly ground black pepper to taste

Kosher salt to taste

Directions:

Use a knife to make a few slits in the leg the on a board mince together oregano, garlic and rosemary.

Stuff the minced mixture into each of the slits then place the lamb inside a roasting pan.

Rub the lamb with some lemon juice and olive oil then then cover using a plastic wrap and refrigerate for about 8 hours or overnight.

Remove from the refrigerator then let the lamb get to room temperature. Season with ground black pepper and salt then get the wood pellet grill preheated to 4000F with lid closed for about 15 minutes.

Roast the lamb for about 30 minutes then reduce the heat to about 3500F and continue cooking until the internal temperature of the lamb gets to 1400F.

Once the lamb is ready, transfer to a cutting board then allow it to rest for about 15 minutes.

Slice and enjoy

Nutrition:

Calories: 251 kCal

Protein: 22 g

Fat: 17 g

20. Lamb Lollipops

Preparation time: 30 minutes

Cooking time: 1 hour

Servings: 4

Ingredients:

Lamb chops – 6

Olive oil – 2 tablespoons

Peeled and seeded mango – 1

Habanero pepper – ½ seeded and chopped

Freshly ground black pepper – ½ teaspoon

Kosher salt – ½ teaspoon

Freshly chopped cilantro – 3 sprigs

Fresh lime juice – 1 tablespoon

Chopped fresh mint – 2 tablespoons

Pepper freshly cracked – ½ teaspoon

Salt – 1 teaspoon

Directions:

Add all of the ingredients for chutney into a food processor then pulse up to desired consistency.

Start the wood pellet grill on smoke as you leave the lid open until the fire comes up. Set the temperature to cook at high for about 15 minutes.

Place the lamb pops over the grill grate then cook for about 30 minutes or until the internal temperature that's inserted at the thickest part of the lamb pop reads 1300F.

Remove from the grill then allow to stay for about 10 minutes.

Sprinkle with some freshly chopped mint then serve and enjoy.

Nutrition:

Calories: 151 kCal

Protein: 21 g

Fat: 13 g

Chapter 5: Poultry Recipes

21. Cured Turkey Drumstick

Preparation time: 20 minutes (additional 14 hours brine / dry)

Cooking time: 2.5 hours to 3 hours

Servings: 3

Ingredients:

Pellets: Hickory, maple

3 fresh or thawed frozen turkey drumsticks

3 tablespoons extra virgin olive oil

Brine component

4 cups of filtered water

¼Cup kosher salt

¼ cup brown sugar

1 tsp garlic powder

Poultry seasoning 1 tsp

1/2 teaspoon red pepper flakes

1 teaspoon pink hardened salt

Directions:

Put the saltwater ingredients in a 1-gallon sealable bag. Add the turkey drumstick to the salt water and refrigerate for 12 hours.

After 12 hours, remove the drumstick from the saline, rinse with cold water, and pat dry with a paper towel.

After 2 hours, increase grill temperature to 325 ° F.

Cooking Time the turkey drumstick at 325 ° F until the internal temperature of the thickest part of each drumstick is 180 ° F with an instant reading digital thermometer.

Place a smoked turkey drumstick under a loose foil tent for 15 minutes before eating.

Nutrition:

Calories: 280

Carbs: 0g

Fat: 13g

Protein: 35g

22. Tailgate Smoked Young Turkey

Preparation time: 20 minutes

Cooking time: 4 to 4 hours 30 minutes

Servings: 8-10

Ingredients:

Pellets: Apple, cherry

1 (10 lb.) fresh or thawed frozen young turkey

6 glasses of extra virgin olive oil with roasted garlic flavor

6 original Yang dry lab or poultry seasonings

Directions:

Remove excess fat and skin from turkey breasts and cavities.

Carefully separate the skin from the turkey breast and a quarter of the leg, leaving the skin intact.

Apply olive oil to the chest, under the skin and on the skin.

Gently rub or season to the chest cavity, under the skin and on the skin.

Set up tailgate wood pellet smoker grill for indirect cooking and smoking. Preheat to 225 ° F using apple or cherry pellets.

Place the turkey on the grill with the chest up.

Suck the turkey for 4-4 hours at 225 ° F until the thickest part of the turkey's chest reaches an internal temperature of 170 ° F and the juice is clear.

Before engraving, place the turkey under a loose foil tent for 20 minutes.

Nutrition:

Calories: 240

Carbs: 27g

Fat: 9g

Protein: 15g

23. Roast Duck A'l Orange

Preparation time: 30 minutes

Cooking time: 2 to 2.5 hours

Servings: 3-4

Ingredients:

Pellet: Optional

1 (5-6 lb.) Frozen Long Island, Beijing, or Canadian ducks

3 tbsp west or 3 tbsp

1 large orange, cut into wedges

Three celery stems chopped into large chunks

Half a small red onion, a quarter

Orange sauce:

2 orange cups

2 tablespoons soy sauce

2 tablespoons orange marmalade

2 tablespoons honey

3g tsp grated raw

Directions:

Remove the jibble from the duck's cavity and neck and retain or discard for another use. Rinse the duck and pat dry with a paper towel.

Remove excess fat from tail, neck, and cavity. Use a sharp scalpel knife tip to pierce the duck's skin entirely, so that it does not penetrate the duck's meat, to help dissolve the fat layer beneath the skin.

Add the seasoning inside the cavity with one cup of rub or seasoning.

Season the outside of the duck with the remaining friction or seasoning.

Fill the cavity with orange wedges, celery and onion. Duck legs are tied with butcher twine to make filling easier. Place the duck breast up on a small rack of shallow roast bread.

To make the sauce, mix the ingredients in the saucepan over low heat and cook until the sauce is thick and syrupy. Set aside and let cool.

Use of wood pellet smokers and grills

Set the wood pellet smoker grill for indirect cooking and use the pellets to preheat to 350 ° F.

Roast the ducks at 350 ° F for 2 hours.

After 2 hours, brush the duck freely with orange sauce.

Roast the orange glass duck for another 30 minutes, making sure that the inside temperature of the thickest part of the leg reaches 165 ° F.

Place duck under loose foil tent for 20 minutes before serving.

Discard the orange wedge, celery, and onion. Serve with a quarter of duck with poultry scissors.

Nutrition:

Calories: 250

Carbs: 7g

Fat: 17g

Protein: 17g

24. Stuffed Smoked Turkey

Preparation time: 1 hour

Cooking time: 3 hours

Servings: 6

Ingredients:

15lb Whole Turkey

1 cup Kozmo's Turkey Brine

Swine Life Miss Grind Rub

14oz Pepperidge Farm Seasoned Bread Cubes

1 lb. Country Sausage

22oz chicken broth

1 cup Granny Smith Apple

1 cup Celery

1 Onion

3 cloves Garlic

1 stick Butter

1 large Egg

2 teaspoon Killer Hogs AP Seasoning

1 teaspoon fresh Rosemary

1 teaspoon fresh Thyme

1 teaspoon fresh Sage

Directions:

Defrost turkey and take giblet and neck. Spot Turkey in XXL plastic zip lock stockpiling percent, add 1 cup Kozmo's Turkey Brine and 1 gallon of water, press the permit a few streams into of sack and close. Spot the turkey in a huge plastic bowl or tote and see it inside the cooler for 24Hrs.

Take the turkey out from the saline answer and permit plentiful fluid to use up away. Air to dry the skin tapping it with a paper towel to take out dampness.

In a big sauté skillet darkish to colored wiener and channel. Leave 1 tablespoon of wiener drippings inside the field and sauté onion, celery, and apple for three to four mins. Include garlic and prepare dinner for a further 2mins.

Splash the skin with cooking shower and season with Killer Hogs AP Seasoning observed by Swine Life Mississippi Grind.

In a large bowl join the bread three to D shapes with a wiener, sautéed combination, liquefied spread, egg, herbs, 1 teaspoon AP flavoring and bird juices. Mix to sign up for and stuff into the pit of the turkey. Tie the legs collectively with butcher twine to keep within the stuffing.

Set up a pellet flame broil for indirect cooking at three hundred levels utilizing a blend of Hickory, Maple, and Cherry wooden pellets for boosting.

Spot the turkey at the smoker and cook till an internal temperature of 165 inside the bosom. Make sure to check the inward temperature of the stuffing too. It likewise needs to arrive at 165 previous serving.

Take the turkey out from the smoker, rest for 15mins before slicing.

Nutrition:

Calories: 221

Carbs: 18g

Fat: 9g

Protein: 18g

25. Herb Buttered Spatchcock Chicken

Preparation time: 10 minutes

Cooking time: 1 hour

Servings: 6-8

Ingredients:

1 stick of butter

2 tbsp. garlic powder

2 tbsp. chipotle chili powder

Thyme

Basil

Directions:

Begin with a sharp butcher blade and start by scoring a line down the center of the spine. When you have your score line, press solidly into the winged creature and cut it down through the center. Rehash the whole procedure on the opposite side. In the wake of evacuating any additional fat, spread the chicken open so it lays level.Set your Grill to 275⁰ and place your chicken on the meshes. Leave the smoker shut for 45 to seal in the juices and take on the smoke.Spot your chicken on a slicing board and permit it to rest for a couple of minutes to secure the entirety of the juices. Wrap up by cutting your chicken for serving and appreciate!

Nutrition: Calories: 337 Carbs: 0g Fat: 20g Protein: 40g

26. Chipotle Style Smoked Whole Turkey

Preparation time: 40min

Cooking time: 3hrs

Servings: 10

Ingredients:

Kosher Salt

Cumin

Adobo Chipotle

Oregano

Granulated Garlic

Chili Paste

Chili Powder

Ancho Chili Powder

Olive Oil Spray

Butter

Whole Turkey (15 lbs.)

Directions:

To begin, take a pointy blade and spatchcock your chook. For those who do not have the foggiest concept of the way to investigate this video for an into profundity explanation.

Once sufficiently prepared, positioned your turkey for your Grilla Grill at normally 275^{0}. Leave it in for approximately 45 to 50mins, at that factor knock the temperature as much as 350^{0} for the closing hour of cooking. These occasions are for a fifteen lbs. fledgling, so change as wishes be for the dimensions of your turkey. Your Thanksgiving chook ought to arrive at an inner temperature of in any occasion 165^{0} for secure utilization.

Nutrition:

Calories: 500

Carbs: 27g

Fat: 27g

Protein: 30g

27. Grilled BBQ Orange Chicken

Preparation time: 10 minutes

Cooking time: 20 minutes

Ingredients:

1 whole 5 to lb. (or larger) chicken

1 24 to oz jar orange marmalade

1 TB fresh ginger

2 TB red pepper flakes

¼ C Grilla AP Rub

3 TB Grilla BBQ Sauce

Directions:

In the occasion that you need to spare prepare dinner time, you may want to start via dispatch to positioning the hen. This will reduce round 20 percentage off of the cook time. In the occasion that you lean closer to the creation of an entire bird depart entirety. Preheat your Grill to 275⁰.

In a bit sauce skillet, melt the orange jelly on low. Include the BBQ sauce and ginger to this mixture.

During the remaining 20mins of cooking, cowl the winged creature with the jelly combination in 10 to 12mins interims. In the occasion that you have some last, that is great—it is outstanding to dunk the meat into on the off chance which you pull the beef from the flying creature.

Nutrition:

Calories: 250

Carbs: 19g

Fat: 7g

Protein: 26g

28. Smoked Turkey Legs

Preparation time: 7 hours

Cooking time: 20min

Servings: 6

Ingredients:

8 Turkey Legs

2 quarts water

1/2 cup Sugar

1/2 cup Killer Hogs AP Rub

2 to 3 Bay leaves

¼ cup Killer Hogs the BBQ Rub

1 cup Killer Hogs Vinegar Sauce

Directions:

In big bowl join water, 1 cup sugar, ¼ cup AP rub, and narrows leaves. Spot the turkey legs into the saline solution arrangement and refrigerate medium-term or possibly 6Hrs.

Spot the legs on the smoker and cook until interior temperature arrives at 155 to 160⁰.

Coating every turkey leg with the vinegar sauce and keep on cooking until the inside temperature arrives at 175⁰ at that point Take from the smoker and rest for 5 to 10mins before serving.

Nutrition:

Calories: 190

Carbs: 1g

Fat: 9g

Protein: 24g

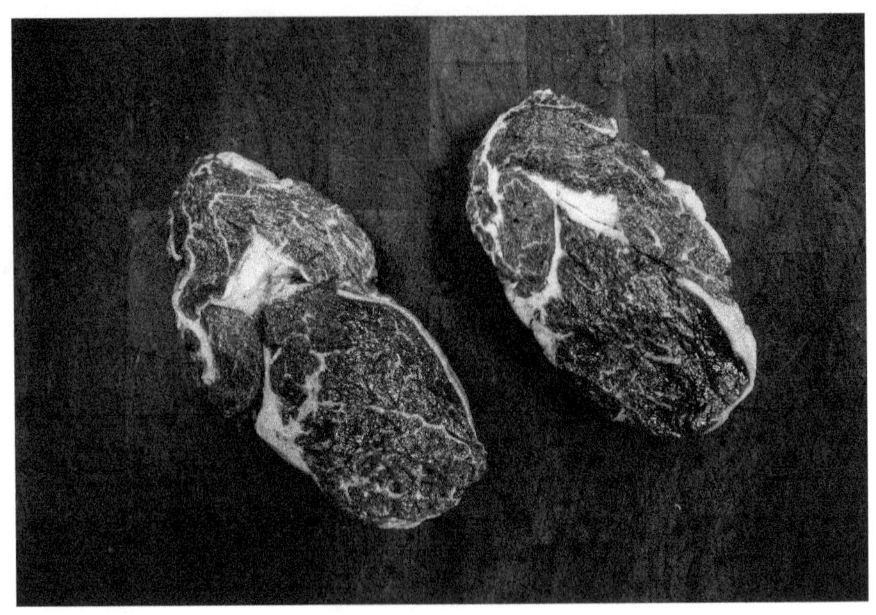

Chapter 6: Seafood Recipes

29. Hot-Smoked Salmon

Preparation time: 15 minutes

Cooking time: 4 to 6 hours

Servings: 4

Ingredients:

Pellet: Hickory

1 (2-pound) half salmon fillet

1 batch Dill Seafood Rub

Directions:

Supply your smoker with wood pellets and follow the manufacturer's specific start-up procedure. Preheat the grill, with the lid closed, to 180°F.

Season the salmon all over with the rub. Using your hands, work the rub into the flesh.

Place the salmon directly on the grill grate, skin-side down, and smoke until its internal temperature reaches 145°F. Remove the salmon from the grill and serve immediately.

Nutrition:

Calories: 227 Carbs: 1g Fat: 15g Protein: 23g

30. Wood-Fired Halibut

Preparation time: 5 minutes

Cooking time: 20 minutes

Servings: 4

Ingredients:

Pellet: Hickory

pound halibut fillet

1 batch Dill Seafood Rub

Directions:

Supply your smoker with wood pellets and follow the manufacturer's specific start-up procedure. Preheat the grill, with the lid closed, to 325°F.

Sprinkle the halibut fillet on all sides with the rub. Using your hands, work the rub into the meat.

Place the halibut directly on the grill grate and grill until its internal temperature reaches 145°F. Remove the halibut from the grill and serve immediately.

Nutrition:

Calories: 320

Carbs: 0g

Fat: 0g Protein: 0g

31. Seared Tuna Steaks

Preparation time: 10 minutes

Cooking time: 10 minutes

Servings: 2

Ingredients:

Pellet: Oak

2 (1½- to 2-inch-thick) tuna steaks

2 tablespoons olive oil

Salt

Freshly ground black pepper

Directions:

Supply your smoker with wood pellets and follow the manufacturer's specific start-up procedure. Preheat the grill, with the lid closed, to 500°F.

Rub the tuna steaks all over with olive oil and season both sides with salt and pepper.

Place the tuna steaks directly on the grill grate and grill for 3 to 5 minutes per side, leaving a pink center. Remove the tuna steaks from the grill and serve immediately.

Nutrition:

Calories: 210 Carbs: 0g Fat: 2g Protein: 49g

32. Barbecued Shrimp

Preparation time: 15 to 30 minutes

Cooking time: 10 minutes

Servings: 4

Ingredients:

Pellet: Mesquite

1 pound peeled and deveined shrimp, with tails on

2 tablespoons olive oil

1 batch Dill Seafood Rub

Soak wooden skewers in water for 30 minutes.

Directions:

Supply your smoker with wood pellets and follow the manufacturer's specific start-up procedure. Preheat the grill, with the lid closed, to 375°F.

Thread 4 or 5 shrimp per skewer.

Coat the shrimp all over with olive oil and season each side of the skewers with the rub.

Place the skewers directly on the grill grate and grill the shrimp for 5 minutes per side. Remove the skewers from the grill and serve immediately.

Nutrition: Calories: 227 Carbs: 7g Fat: 5g Protein: 37g

33. Cajun-Blackened Shrimp

Preparation time: 10 minutes

Cooking time: 20 minutes

Servings: 4

Ingredients:

Pellet: Alder

1 pound peeled and deveined shrimp, with tails on

1 batch Cajun Rub

8 tablespoons (1 stick) butter

¼ cup Worcestershire sauce

Directions:

Supply your smoker with wood pellets and follow the manufacturer's specific start-up procedure. Preheat the grill, with the lid closed, to 450°F and place a cast-iron skillet on the grill grate. Wait about 10 minutes after your grill has reached temperature, allowing the skillet to get hot.

Meanwhile, season the shrimp all over with the rub.

When the skillet is hot, place the butter in it to melt. Once the butter melts, stir in the Worcestershire sauce.

Add the shrimp and gently stir to coat. Smoke-braise the shrimp for about 10 minutes per side, until opaque and cooked through. Remove the shrimp from the grill and serve immediately.

Nutrition:

Calories: 320

Carbs: 17g

Fat: 10g

Protein: 39g

34. Oysters in Shell

Preparation time: 5 minutes

Cooking time: 20 minutes

Servings: 4

Ingredients:

Pellet: Oak

8 medium oysters, unopened, in the shell, rinsed and scrubbed

1 batch Lemon Butter Mop for Seafood

Directions:

Supply your smoker with wood pellets and follow the manufacturer's specific start-up procedure. Preheat the grill, with the lid closed, to 375°F.

Place the unopened oysters directly on the grill grate and grill for about 20 minutes, or until the oysters are done and their shells open.

Discard any oysters that do not open. Shuck the remaining oysters, transfer them to a bowl, and add the mop. Serve immediately.

Nutrition:

Calories: 50

Carbs: 3g

Fat: 2g Protein: 6g

35. Cajun Catfish

Preparation time: 15 minutes

Cooking time: 15 minutes

Servings: 2

Ingredients:

Pellet: Mesquite

2½ pounds catfish fillets

2 tablespoons olive oil

1 batch Cajun Rub

Directions:

Supply your smoker with wood pellets and follow the manufacturer's specific start-up procedure. Preheat the grill, with the lid closed, to 300°F.

Coat the catfish fillets all over with olive oil and season with the rub. Using your hands, work the rub into the flesh.

Place the fillets directly on the grill grate and smoke until their internal temperature reaches 145°F. Remove the catfish from the grill and serve immediately.

Nutrition:

Calories: 210

Carbs: 0g Fat: 10g Protein: 27g

36. Grilled King Crab Legs

Preparation time: 5 minutes

Cooking time: 10 minutes

Servings: 4

Ingredients:

Pellet: Alder

8 cooked king crab legs

1 batch Lemon Butter Mop for Seafood

Directions:

Supply your smoker with wood pellets and follow the manufacturer's specific start-up procedure. Preheat the grill, with the lid closed, to 325°F.

Place the crab legs directly on the grill grate and grill for 10 minutes, flipping once after 5 minutes. Serve the crab with the mop on the side for dipping.

Nutrition:

Calories: 80

Carbs: 0g

Fat: 2g

Protein: 18g

37. Lobster Tail

Preparation time: 15 minutes

Cooking time: 25 minutes

Servings: 2

Ingredients:

Pellet: Hickory

2 lobster tails

Salt

Freshly ground black pepper

1 batch Lemon Butter Mop for Seafood

Directions:

Supply your smoker with wood pellets and follow the manufacturer's specific start-up procedure. Preheat the grill, with the lid closed, to 375°F.

Using kitchen shears, slit the top of the lobster shells, through the center, nearly to the tail. Once cut, expose as much meat as you can through the cut shell.Season the lobster tails all over with salt and pepper.Place the tails directly on the grill grate and grill until their internal temperature reaches 145°F. Remove the lobster from the grill and serve with the mop on the side for dipping.

Nutrition: Calories: 127 Carbs: 3g Fat: 2g Protein: 23g

38. Barbecued Scallops

Preparation time: 10 minutes

Cooking time: 10 minutes

Servings: 4

Ingredients:

Pellet: Mesquite

pound large scallops

2 tablespoons olive oil

1 batch Dill Seafood Rub

Directions:

Supply your smoker with wood pellets and follow the manufacturer's specific start-up procedure. Preheat the grill, with the lid closed, to 375°F.

Coat the scallops all over with olive oil and season all sides with the rub.

Place the scallops directly on the grill grate and grill for 5 minutes per side. Remove the scallops from the grill and serve immediately.

Nutrition:

Calories: 100

Carbs: 3g

Fat: 1g Protein: 17g

Chapter 7: Vegetable Recipes

39. Grilled Fingerling Potato Salad

Preparation time:15 mins

Cooking time:15 mins

Servings:6-8

Ingredients:

Pellet: hardwood, pecan

1-1/2 lbs. Fingerling potatoes cut in half lengthwise

10 scallions

2/3 cup Evo (extra virgin olive oil), divided use

2 tbsp rice vinegar

2 tsp lemon juice

1 small jalapeno, sliced

2 tsp kosher salt

Directions:

When ready to cook, set temperature to High and preheat, lid closed for 15 minutes.

Brush the scallions with the oil and place on the grill. Cook until lightly charred, about 2-3 minutes. Remove and let cool. Once the scallions have cooled, slice and set aside.

Brush the Fingerlings with oil (reserving 1/3 cup for later use), then salt and pepper. Place cut side down on the grill until cooked through, about 4-5 minutes.

In a bowl, whisk the remaining 1/3 cup olive oil, rice vinegar, salt, and lemon juice, then mix in the scallions, potatoes, and sliced jalapeno.

Season with salt and pepper and serve. Enjoy!

Nutrition:

Calories: 270

Carbs: 18g

Fat: 18g

Protein: 3g

40. Smoked Jalapeño Poppers

Preparation time:15 mins

Cooking time:60 mins

Servings:4-6

Ingredients:

Pellet: hardwood, mesquite

12 medium jalapeños

6 slices bacon, cut in half

8 oz cream cheese, softened

1 cup cheese, grated

2 tbsp Traeger pork & poultry rub

Directions:

When ready to cook, set temperature to 180°F and preheat, lid closed for 15 minutes.

Slice the jalapeños in half lengthwise. Scrape out any seeds and ribs with a small spoon or paring knife.

Mix softened cream cheese with Traeger Pork & Poultry rub and grated cheese.

Spoon mixture onto each jalapeño half. Wrap with bacon and secure with a toothpick.

Place the jalapeños on a rimmed baking sheet. Place on grill and smoke for 30 minutes.

Increase the grill temperature to 375°F and cook an additional 30 minutes or until bacon is cooked to desired doneness. Serve warm, enjoy!

Nutrition:

Calories: 280

Carbs: 24g

Fat: 19g

Protein: 4g

41. Grilled Veggie Sandwich

Preparation time:30 mins

Cooking time:30 mins

Servings:4-6

Ingredients:

Pellet: hardwood, pecan

Smoked hummus

1-1/2 cups chickpeas

1/3 cup tahini

1 tbsp minced garlic

2 tbsp olive oil

1 tsp kosher salt

4 tbsp lemon juice

Grilled veggie sandwich

1 small eggplant, sliced into strips

1 small zucchini, sliced into strips

1 small yellow squash, sliced into strips

2 large portobello mushrooms

Olive oil

Salt and pepper to taste

2 heirloom tomatoes, sliced

1 bunch basil, leaves pulled

4 ciabatta buns

1/2 cup ricotta

Juice of 1 lemon

1 garlic clove minced

Salt and pepper to taste

Directions:

When ready to cook, set temperature to 180°F and preheat, lid closed for 15 minutes.

In the bowl of a food processor, combine smoked chickpeas, tahini, garlic, olive oil, salt and lemon juice and process until mixed well but not completely smooth. Transfer to a bowl and reserve.

Increase grill temp to high (400-500°F).

While the veggies are cooking combine the ricotta, lemon juice, garlic, salt and pepper in a small bowl.Cut the ciabatta buns in half and open them up. Spread hummus on one side and ricotta on the other. Stack the grilled veggies and top with tomatoes and basil. Enjoy!

Nutrition: Calories: 376 Carbs: 57g Fat: 16g Protein: 10g

42. Roasted Pickled Beets

Preparation time:15 mins Cooking time:10 mins

Servings:8-12 Ingredients:

Pellet: hardwood, maple

6 medium beets, preferably candy cane beets, stem ends trimmed

1 cup high-quality red wine vinegar

1/2 cup sugar or honey

1 1/2 tsp. Coarse or kosher salt

1 cup water

6-8 whole cloves

5 whole peppercorns

2 pieces star anise

1 cinnamon stick, broken in half

Directions:

Make a foil pouch large enough to enclose the beets. Poke a few holes in the top to allow steam to escape.Put the cloves, peppercorns, star anise, and cinnamon in a clean lidded jar, such as a canning jar. Add the beets to the jar. Pour the hot brine over the beets. Put the lid on the jar. Cool the beets to room temperature, then refrigerate for 3 to 5 days before serving.

Nutrition:

Calories: 65 Carbs: 17g Fat: 0g Protein: 0g

43. Smoked Healthy Cabbage

Preparation time: 10 minutes

Cooking time: 2 hours

Servings: 5

Ingredients:

Pellet: maple pellets

1 head cabbage, cored

4 tablespoons butter

2 tablespoons rendered bacon fat

1 chicken bouillon cube

1 teaspoon fresh ground black pepper

1 garlic clove, minced

Directions:

Pre-heat your smoker to 240 degrees Fahrenheit using your preferred woodFill the hole of your cored cabbage with butter, bouillon cube, bacon fat, pepper and garlicWrap the cabbage in foil about two-thirds of the way up Make sure to leave the top open

Transfer to your smoker rack and smoke for 2 hours

Unwrap and enjoy!

Nutrition: Calories: 231 Fats: 10g Carbs: 26g Fiber: 1g

44. Beer Smoked Cabbage with Garlic Rub

Preparation Time: 40 minutes

Cooking Time: 3 hours

Servings: 10

Ingredients:

Whole cabbages (3-lb., 1.4-kg.)

Olive oil – 3 tablespoons

Garlic powder – 2 teaspoons

Salt – ¼ teaspoon

Chili powder – ¼ teaspoon

Ground cinnamon – ½ teaspoon

Beer – 1 can

Directions:

Combine garlic powder, salt, chili powder, and ground cinnamon in a bowl.

Drizzle olive oil over the spices then mix well.

Rub the spice mixture over the cabbage and in between the cabbage leaves.

Next, plug the wood pellet smoker then fill the hopper with the wood pellet. Turn the switch on.

Set the wood pellet smoker for indirect heat then adjust the temperature to 275°F (135°C).

Place the seasoned cabbage on a sheet of aluminum foil then wrap the cabbage. Let the top of the cabbage open.

Pour beer over the cabbage then place it in the wood pellet smoker. Smoke the cabbage for 3 hours, until tender.

Once it is done, remove the smoked cabbage from the wood pellet smoker and unwrap it.

Cut the smoked cabbage into wedges then serve.

Enjoy!

Nutrition:

Calories: 300

Carbs: 70g

Fat: 2g

Protein: 18g

45. Smoked Asparagus with Sesame Aroma

Preparation Time: 20 minutes

Cooking Time: 1 hour

Servings: 10

Ingredients:

Asparagus (2-lbs., 0.9-kg.)

Sesame oil – 2 tablespoons

Lemon juice – 2 tablespoons

Grated lemon zest – ¼ teaspoon

Garlic powder – 1 teaspoon

Salt – ½ teaspoon

Pepper – ¼ teaspoon

Directions:

Combine grated lemon zest, garlic powder, salt, and pepper in a bowl then drizzle lemon juice and sesame oil over the spices. Mix well.

Cut and trim the asparagus then rub with the spice mixture.

Next, wrap the seasoned asparagus with aluminum foil then set aside.

After that, plug the wood pellet smoker then fill the hopper with the wood pellet. Turn the switch on.

Set the wood pellet smoker for indirect heat then adjust the temperature to 225°F (107°C).

Place the wrapped asparagus in the wood pellet smoker and smoke for an hour, until tender.

Once it is done, remove the smoked asparagus from the wood pellet smoker then transfer to a serving dish.

Serve and enjoy.

Nutrition:

Calories: 250

Carbs: 26g

Fat: 9g

Protein: 19g

Chapter 8: Sides

46. Bacon Cheddar Slider

Preparation time: 30 minutes

Cooking time: 15 minutes

Servings: 6-10

Ingredients:

Pellet: Optional

1-pound ground beef (80% lean)

1/2 teaspoon of garlic salt

1/2 teaspoon salt

1/2 teaspoon of garlic

1/2 teaspoon onion

1/2 teaspoon black pepper

6 bacon slices, cut in half

½Cup mayonnaise

2 teaspoons of creamy wasabi (optional)

6 (1 oz) sliced sharp cheddar cheese, cut in half (optional)

Sliced red onion

½Cup sliced kosher dill pickles

12 mini breads sliced horizontally

Ketchup

Directions:

Place ground beef, garlic salt, seasoned salt, garlic powder, onion powder and black hupe pepper in a medium bowl.

Set up a wood pellet smoker grill for direct cooking to use griddle accessories.

Spray a cooking spray on the griddle cooking surface for best non-stick results.

Preheat wood pellet smoker grill to 350 ° F using selected pellets. Griddle surface should be approximately 400 ° F.

Grill the putty for 3-4 minutes each until the internal temperature reaches 160 ° F.

Place a small amount of mayonnaise mixture, a slice of red onion, and a hamburger pate in the lower half of each roll. Pickled slices, bacon and ketchup

Nutrition:

Calories: 80

Carbs: 0g

Fat: 5g

Protein: 0g

47. Apple Wood Smoked Cheese

Preparation time: 1 hour 15 minutes

Cooking time: 3 hours

Servings: 10

Ingredients:

Pellet: Apple

Gouda

Sharp cheddar

Very sharp 3-year cheddar

Monterey Jack

Pepper jack

Swiss

Directions:

Preheat the wood pellet smoker grill to 180 ° F or use apple pellets and smoke settings, if any, to get a milder smoke flavor.

Place the cheese on a Teflon-coated fiberglass non-stick grill mat and let cool for 2 hours.

Leave the cheese on the counter for one hour to form a fragile skin or crust, which acts as a heat barrier, but allows smoke to penetrate.

After labeling the smoked cheese with a vacuum seal, refrigerate for 2 weeks or more, then smoke will permeate, and the cheese flavor will become milder.

Nutrition:

Calories: 102

Carbs: 0g

Fat: 9g

Protein: 6g

Chapter 9: Snacks, Dessert and Extras

48. Blackberry Pie

Preparation time: 10 minutes

Cooking time: 40 minutes

Servings: 8

Ingredients:

Butter, for greasing

½ c. all-purpose flour

½ c. milk

Two pints blackberries

Two c. sugar, divided

One box refrigerated piecrusts

One stick melted butter

One stick of butter

Vanilla ice cream

Directions:

Add wood pellets to your smoker and follow your cooker's startup procedure. Preheat your smoker, with your lid closed, until it reaches 375.

Unroll the second pie crust and lay it over the skillet.

Lower the lid and smoke for 15 to 20 minutes or until it is browned and bubbly.

Serve the hot pie with some vanilla ice cream.

Nutrition:

Calories: 100

Carbs: 10g

Fat: 0g

Protein: 15g

49. S'mores Dip

Preparation time: 0 minutes

Cooking time: 15 minutes

Servings: 6-8

Ingredients:

12 ounces semisweet chocolate chips

¼ c. milk

Two T. melted salted butter

16 ounces marshmallows

Apple wedges

Graham crackers

Directions:

Add wood pellets to your smoker and follow your cooker's startup procedure. Preheat your smoker, with your lid closed, until it reaches 450.

Put a cast iron skillet on your grill and add in the milk and melted butter. Stir together for a minute.Cover, and let it smoke for five to seven minutes. The marshmallows should be toasted lightly.Take the skillet off the heat and serve with apple wedges and graham crackers.

Nutrition: Calories: 90 Carbs: 15g Fat: 3g Protein: 1g

50. Bacon Chocolate Chip Cookies

Preparation time: 10 minutes

Cooking time: 30 minutes

Servings: 24

Ingredients:

8 slices cooked and crumbled bacon

2 ½ t. apple cider vinegar

One t. vanilla

Two c. semisweet chocolate chips

Two room temp eggs

1 ½ t. baking soda

One c. granulated sugar

½ t. salt

2 ¾ c. all-purpose flour

One c. light brown sugar

1 ½ stick softened butter

Directions:

Mix together the flour, baking soda, and salt.

Cream the sugar and the butter together. Lower the speed. Add in the eggs, vinegar, and vanilla.

Still on low, slowly add in the flour mixture, bacon pieces, and chocolate chips.

Add wood pellets to your smoker and follow your cooker's startup procedure. Preheat your smoker, with your lid closed, until it reaches 375.

Place some parchment on a baking sheet and drop a teaspoonful of cookie batter on the baking sheet. Let them cook on the grill,

covered, for approximately 12 minutes or until they are browned. Enjoy.

Nutrition:

Calories: 167

Carbs: 21g

Fat: 9g

Protein: 2g

Conclusion

Grilling summer season never gets to an end, especially if you call yourself a pit master down your heart. Whether you love grilling with your friends or family in your backyard or even if you want to grill by yourself; you would want an innovative and creative grilling technique. Yet, it is challenging sometimes and extremely tough to use a gas or wood grill because of the enormous mess and the cleaning process that will exhaust your and prevent you from enjoying grilling the way you want. And other times, even using your favorite grill cannot give you the results you want neither gives you the flavors you are looking for.

Have you ever wondered about what you can do to resolve this and make grilling one of the memorable experiences you will ever get? Just imagine finding the grill that combines the versatility, the convenience, and the ease of using a gas grill and the flavor of hardwood and smoke into your grilled ingredients? Does it sound like a dream come true? Pellet grill combines the advantages of gas grill and hardwood barbecue to offer you an incredible taste only with the use of your favorite type of pellets like apple or oak pellets. Using pellet smoker or grills will not only offer you a great versatility, but also a great pack of flavor you have never imagined you would get. Does it sound too good to be true? Well, the unmatched flavor pellet grills offer is so real, and you will be surprised at how easy pellet grills are simple to use, to clean and to cook a wide variety of food ingredients.

Pellet smoker and grills can play the role of ovens, grills and you will be amazed at how practical this type of pellet grills is. Now that you have finished reading this cookbook, you learned how to properly use the revolutionary and creative cooking device known as pellet grills as well as various and useful tips. Pellet grills are only fueled by pellets which will make your experience healthier and safer. You can infuse the flavor you want through the type of pellets you want.

As you can see from these recipes, the world of smoking is only as limited as your imagination! Sweet, savory, vegetable, mineral, meat- you can smoke almost anything. As you get more comfortable with these recipes, feel free to start experimenting on your own. The basic principles hold, but your taste buds can drive you. You will be surprised that the wood pellet smoker and grill look exactly like a classic smoker and that the Pellet grill perfectly fits into outdoor areas and outdoor kitchens alike. If you have guests, you don't have to worry anymore because now you will be able to enjoy chit chats with them while your food is being grilled thanks to the Pellet grills.

CPSIA information can be obtained
at www.ICGtesting.com
Printed in the USA
BVHW051554090321
602118BV00004B/378